I0148042

8th House Publishing
Montreal, Canada

First Edition

Cover Art: Elk, 2010. Watercolour, ink, and coloured pencil on hot pressed 90 lb watercolour paper © 2010 Tara Chartrand
Cover Photo of K. Gandhar Chakravarty © Anna Waclawek
Design by 8th House Publishing

A CIP catalogue record for this book is available from Library and Archives Canada.

LIBRARY AND ARCHIVES CANADA
CATALOGUING IN PUBLICATION

Maple Vedas / Chakravarty, K. Gandhar (1979 -)
ISBN 978-1-926716-05-3 (pb)

1. Literature--Poetry. I. Chakravarty, K. Gandhar. Maple Vedas II. Title

8th House Publishing
Montreal, Canada

Maple Vedas

by

K. Gandhar Chakravarty

8TH HOUSE PUBLISHING · MONTREAL, CANADA

PRAISE FOR MAPLE VEDAS

***

Rana Bose, *Author*

"Gandhar has messed with identity and time in a Puckish and magical manner.... Like in A Midsummer Night's Dream, there is a primary motivation to lose one's individuality and deconstruct reality. Gandhar has done that with excellence while merging the maple with the tulsi leaf.... classic."

~

Let me just take a deep breath and exhale first. K. Gandhar Chakravarty, a Montrealer of Indian origins, has come up with a 38-page poetry book, close on the winged heels of his earlier production Kolkata Dreams from the same publisher. Let me now take a deeper breath. This young man – traveller, musician, poet, band leader, religion aficionado (no, not nut job, please, just an analyser of the spirits of godliness from Ganeshism to Rastafari) – has come up with a series of thinly concealed poetic barbs that gnash, lash, caress, frolic, froth and then release you into the humdrum streets of Montreal and the green Canadian wilderness in the company of disreputable Hindu gods who would have been smoking something by now if they were still around. Another deep breath. So, in a mild but genial and intelligent manner, Gandhar has messed with identity and time in a Puckish and magical manner. Combining insects, worms, animals, asses, monkeys, seagulls, mantis, monarch butterflies, crabs, and scorpions, he has created a book of short green poems that combine the dour mapleness of Canada with the stoned madness of Indian and Buddhist aphorisms.

Almost like a narcotic dream at times, there is a blurring of fantasy and fairy reality as the Hindu god Shiva, with his dreadlocks flying, boards a number 24 bus on Sherbrooke Street in Montreal and watches butterflies and dragonflies, while his mistress goddess Parvati, leans on him and addresses him with cute Indian female caution:

> *Thus Parvati whispered sweetly to Shiva:*

"One day, if you smoke too much,
you might fall down."

One can hear the sing-song tonality seeping out of the lines.

Irrational love, irrational politics, irrational philosophizing are corner stones of subcontinental religions like Hinduism, Buddhism, or Jainism. That is why loss of personal identity is fundamental to explaining why the so-called Eastern religions mix humour with irrationality in the hopes of future bliss. Either that or you ingest spliff after spliff. Like in A Midsummer Night's Dream, there is a primary motivation to lose one's individuality and deconstruct reality. Gandhar has done that with excellence while merging the maple with the tulsi leaf.

The inside cover page states "To be read aloud". Is that a threat or warning? So I started reading it aloud and naturally there are sections where one is beside oneself. Deconstructing religion and addressing Bengali infatuation for certain Hindu idols like the "butter pilfering" Krishna and a bonged-out Shiva make for memorable moments. Gandhar should know that messing with religion gets fatwas unleashed. But here he is on safe territory, because subcontinental religions "swim in the void," so to speak and do not always unleash fanatics.

So here are some classic moments from the book:

Shiva to a mallard in Lafontaine Park!

—Hare duck!
I love you so much.

And:

One day, Hanuman took a day off.

He spent his holiday in the Bush Lands of the West,
leaving his mace behind.

As Krishna becomes Chrisna towards the end, here is some scorching Canadian multiethnic perversity:

Shiva hopped a Vancouver taxi one evening
after smoking a joint at an old friend's.

As they rode through the village,
the driver spoke in a thick Turkish accent,
his throat chaffed from cigarette smoke:

"You see these?

"These are the gays...

"This is their... territory."

Shiva, stoned, knew better than to protest

In Maple Vedas, there is a unique irony and deconstructive explosiveness that passes you by like a mild thump in the hills. A great follow-up to Kolkata Dreams.

***

Allison Adelle Hedge Coke, *Poet*

"An amazing display of talent, Chakravarty synthesizes life and times through transmigrations for the beautiful secrets and freedom offered there. The branch of the Maple Vedas extend to a musical fifth, an opus, a poetic Smriti, where we wind ourselves into hearing position by the strum and tone of the turning page, seeking our own genus through the words of surrounding companions—delightfully charged!"

~

In sacred knowledge, parallels prophesy universal wisdom, where information belies pedantry, erudition, and reveals itself through awareness, exchange, and experience, syllogistic and inductive. Hindu Sanskrit philosophy, ritual orality, recites seers' Vedic knowledge by Rig Veda, Sama Veda, Yajur Veda, Atharva Veda ... in their culminations and singularities, the parallels portray knowns, at once, simple and immense. K. Gandhar Chakravarty unfolds Vedic in verse, in a karmic journey to green maple, sugar maple and pine, venturing on foot, on wings, on the back of moose, swimming, canoeing, wandering throughout the eastern lands of the northern North, New Foundland, Niagara, and westward to Vancouver. All along the while, opening concealed fruits evident in the chance meetings between Hanuman, Shiva, Chrisna, Rhanna, Kali ... and Moose, Mallard, Dragonfly, Wasp, Loon, Grasshopper, until their propensities disclose tenets the poet hears and jointly speaks to. Thus leading us to accompany the seeking on this image-ridden journey into solar lights shining only for us, versified, and swimming for all time, here and now. An amazing display of talent, Chakravarty synthesizes life and times through transmigrations for the beautiful secrets and freedom offered there. The branch of the Maple Vedas extend to a musical fifth, an opus, a poetic Smriti, where we wind ourselves into hearing position by the strum and tone of the turning page, seeking our own genus through the words of surrounding companions—delightfully charged!

For the little Indian in all of us...

Maple Vedas

To be read aloud

Swan in the Void, 2010.
Watercolour, ink, and coloured pencil on hot pressed 90 lb watercolour paper, 5" x 6".
TARA CHARTRAND

I.

Before Lord Krishna danced with the maidens,
        he was but a child,
        pilfering potted butter.

As he sang to the swan upon the pond,
        his voice became clear.

"Swan, tell me a story about your birth."

—When I first opened my eyes,
        there was only darkness,
        so I shut my eyes in fear.

—No longer was I nothing;
        still I swam in the void.

II.

One day, in the lotus garden,
in the shade of a banyan tree,
Shiva lounged with his wife,
sipping lassi and munching ripe mangoes,
her small head resting on his strong white chest,
her soft dark hair fluttering in the gentle breeze.

Shiva sat up and reached for his chillum.

Parvati shuffled,
        then rested her head in her palm
        upon her crook'd arm.

She gazed up at her husband as he puffed.

Thus Parvati whispered sweetly to Shiva:

"One day, if you smoke too much,
        you might fall down."

Flight, 2010.
Watercolour, ink, and coloured pencil on hot pressed 90 lb watercolour paper, 5" x 6".
TARA CHARTRAND

III.

A baby pigeon tumbled from the roof slats,
        into the courtyard below.

A young boy asked Krishna
        what they should do.

"Nothing," replied the boy in blue.

—Why not? said the other.

—If we do not lift this bird
        back to its home,
        it may die.

"But if you lift him back,
        it may never learn to fly."

IV.

Hanuman, you silly monkey,
the garden is nestled next your door.

Just push to let it in.

~

One day, Hanuman took a day off.

He spent his holiday in the Bush Lands of the West,
leaving his mace behind.

Crunching snow, monkey pawed,
He gazed at colossal pine, fir, and spruce,
chancing upon a giant brown dull-horned beast
swinging its armoury at the branches of a bayberry bush
shadowed by a yellow birch.

He snapped the brittle branches
with little effort.

"Tell me, sir. What is your name?" asked Hanu.

—Mister… I am known as Mooshkr.

"Sir, Moose, may I ride upon thee?"

Hanuman & The Moose, 2009.
Watercolour and Gouache, 6" x 9".
COLLEEN MacISAAC

—Of course, you may,
        for I sense your honour.

Thus they parted, God and Beast as one,
        crunching through the snow-laden forest.

~

"Sir, Moose, upon what lands do we now tread?"

—I know not what they are called… oohkr…
        my small wiry friend,
        but in time
        people refer to this old land
        as new foundhkr.

"Sir, Moose, do you prophesy?"

—No sir, monkey-god…
        but I will rise again
        from generation to generation,
        my spirit wandering through these thick forests;
        thus it is already foretoldhkr.

—One day, your next-door neighbours
        shall claim this land as their own… oohkr.

V.

"I wander through this cemetery,
 where poppies never bloom,
 amongst forgotten soldiers
 laid beneath
 grey assembly line tombs.

"I ask a groundhog
 nibbling on an acorn
 by a gravestone:

'How long will monuments linger?'

"He hops back into his hole.

"I try to dream of death,
 but every time I close my eyes,
 a car zooms by,
 rumbling over the dead.

"Rank before name,
 each grave the same,
 but for one ungrounded,
 balanced on a brother.

'Oh, groundhog, where have you been?'

—Just underground,
        having tea,
        a deceased corporal and me.

—Did you see that red one go by,
        rumbling over the dead?

—Couldn't they walk
        to see Granma instead?"

~

"Ah-tension. Ah-ten-hut."

"Tension. Ten-hut,"
        blithered the corporal,
        one eye hanging out its socket.

Down hops the groundhog for tea.

—I hope you made some for me.

"Oh, groundhog, where have you been?
        I've been raising an army."

—Corporal, the only thing you should conquer
        with those decaying, worm-beaten limbs,
        is your eye, back to its socket.

Death, 2010.
Gouache, 14" x 14".
CHRIS DYER

“Oh, pardon me.

“How embarrassing.

“Allow me to replace it,
    dear groundhog.”

But as he lifted the sphere
    back towards his skull,
    the thread snapped
    and down plopped the eyeball
    into his tea-cup.

Silence
    and the groundhog blinks stunned.

“Oh, I’ve made such a mess!

“And after all that fuss.

“Just stay a moment,
    and I’ll clean it all up.”

But the groundhog could bear no more,
    and turned his tail up.

VI.

Sometimes Ganesha's trunk would grow so long,
it would curl halfway round the world.

On this day, he followed his nose to a flat land far far away.

~

"The forests of my land are overgrown,
and I shall wish for that again one day.

"But today, I must seek some flat terrain upon which to trumpet my song."

Thus, Ganesha followed his trunk to a flat land far far away,
not yet blonde as wheat,
but vital green bursting
yellow, indigo, magenta, persimmon, ecru, fuchsia, rose, and violet.

"Here my trumpet's call bounces not
against the countless trunks of the great banyan trees,
but rolls across the plains, carried upon the wind."

As He ambled forth,
Ganesha chanced upon one equally wise,
a small brown gopher, one hundredth His size.

Creation Ganeesh, 2010.
Ink and Photoshop, 30" x 8".
CHRIS DYER

—Ganesha, asked the gopher,
        when will it end?

"When a hanged man is found shackled;
        when the knight who rides the white horse
        becomes the shepherd who feeds the white lamb."

VII.

Once, after a tempest, the rightful monarch Prospero
released his airy spirit Ariel from bondage.

But on this day, it would be Chrisna who released the monarch
with wings of amber and black.

Outside the doors of a glass green house,
Chrisna gently opened the small wax-coated pouch,
the frigid imago sleeping inside.

With a few flutters,
the monarch drowsily drifted upon His shoulder.

"Fly, fly, my son, until you reign these lands,
from the Great Lakes to the Oyamel forests,
as they are rightfully yours.

"May your kin return next Spring;
now, I release thee."

VIII.

As Shiva stood inside the 24 bus on Sherbrooke Street,
his joints aligned with the spirit of the machine,
he gazed at a white dandelion puff gliding through, drifting by
a Buddhist monk in red and white sneakers, pausing
to circle just once over a violet left shoulder pad, finally
slinging itself back towards the light outside.

~

This time it was a butterfly,
black with red spots.

She just glided in like a dandelion puff,
startling the lady beside Him;
and as the driver tapped the brakes,
the butterfly found her way out a window crack
on the driver's side.

~

Now, a dragonfly, shimmering electric blue,
that popped its head in just to have a look,
and flew out again into the shade of a bush.

But as the bus lurched to part,
the dragonfly was quick to dart
back inside,
gliding right by Shiva's mane,
finally settling down in the rear.

And as Shiva played with the straps of his knapsack,
he noticed a wasp upon the front pole,
acting droll,
fiddling its wing.

IX.

"I followed the ravine flowing through a sparse wood,
    which brought me to an ancient spot,
    nestled now
    between highway and construction lot.

"I gazed up,
    surprised by His stature,
    no different from His kin.

"The squirrel god, gold and brown,
    spake from the limbs of a green maple:

—We are of the same maker.

"I turned, humbled,
    as a honey bee landed on my finger."

Shiva & The Mallard, 2009.
Watercolour and Gouache, 6" x 9".
COLLEEN MacISAAC

X.

The mallard sits proud upon Lafontaine pond
          shining royal green flecked with black,
          its sky blue eyeball blinking back.

"Shiva," spake the mallard.

"You sneaky devil.

"You have snuck into those bushes
          to have yourself a tinkle."

—*Hare* duck!
          I love you so much.

—May I unclip your wings?

"But Shiva,
          if you gave me back my wings,
          I might fly off.

"Then who would gaze upon me?"

XI.

Chrisna explored Orford one day.

He boarded a canoe with Rhanna,
        his eternal love.

They slipped into the great pond,
        flanked by loon and great blue heron;
        gently they paddled together.

They gazed as the loon would dive,
        for minutes at a time,
        submerged.

After several such bobbings,
        the loon later emerged
        beside the small vessel.

—Couououould
        youououou
        keaeaeaep
        thieieis plaeaeaeaece
        iaiain miaiaiaiaind?

Chrisna Canoeing, 2009.
Watercolour and Gouache, 6" x 9".
COLLEEN MacISAAC

As they tried to respond,
        the loon dove beneath them,
        gliding out of sight,
        perhaps in search of dessert.

Then a great blue heron landed on the canoe's ridge,
        talons scraping ever so slightly,
        setting the starboard slightly lower than the port.

—Fair travellers,
        how do you fare?

"Well, we've been entranced by the loon over there,
        now blessed by your presence."

—'Tis nothing, my dears.

—'Tis us who are blessed to have two such as you here,
        gentle folks who value this space.

—I must leave you now;
        enjoy the day.

Thus, Chrisna and Rhanna
        continued to paddle for some time,
        before they set the canoe on a beach,
        leaving it as they dined.

They ventured on foot,
	through narrow paths,
	among sugar maple and pine,
	pausing here and there to enjoy the smells.

Finally, they spotted a doe and her two fawns,
	so close,
	but with no care.

Lime Girl, 2010.
Watercolour, ink and coloured pencil on hot pressed 90 lb watercolour paper, 4" x 6".
TARA CHARTRAND

XII.

"Oh, old wrinkled lime,
 old wrinkled lime,
 do you have some juice left for me?

"I will cut you to see what's inside,
 and yes, you seem so dry.

"But we will try
 and squeeze out what essence is left;
 a few drops here and a few drops there,
 and from one quarter gushed even a bit of a stream.

"Thanks for waiting for me."

XIII.

One day on Mont Royal,
Chrisna chanced upon a cop sitting atop a dark brown horse,
its eyes glistening black.

"May I ride upon your horse, sir?"
chimed the child divine.

—Yes, my love.
I implore you.

Thus Chrisna danced with Chenresi once more.

They galloped through the far reaches of that baby mountain,
where folks seldom tread,
then trotted down paths long forgotten,
the ones that sometimes vanish when you're not there.

After that, they emerged from the forest,
God and Beast, as one.

Chrisna Rides, 2009.
Watercolour and Gouache, 6" x 9".
COLLEEN MacISAAC

XIV.

A crab and a scorpion
struggle amongst grains
on a white sandy beach.

Claw to claw,
neither would succumb,
the scorpion's stinger unable to pierce
the crab's hard shell.

A fisherman chanced upon the scene
and asked:

"Why do you fight each other?"

Pausing, neither crab nor scorpion
could manage a response.

"Instead of clawing each other,
and wasting breath,
don't you see that claws can build instead?"

Now the two hardened warriors knew love,
        and started to look around.

—Pray, crab, what can we make with sand and shells?

So they dug out a foundation,
        then built up walls of shell and sand,
        and roofs of palm.

From time to time,
        they dance in the flicker of candlelight
        as it bounces along the castle halls.

XV.

“Many holy ones have walked here before me,
pausing to ponder still inuksuit,
stone men that guide the way.

“I sit amongst these still travellers,
sensing their fragile strength against the wind,
stone upon stone,
glued by gravity.

“From the silence,
a chipmunk emerges.

"He smiles at me,
        while munching a nut.

—How now? he said.

"As the chipmunk squirrels away,
        the faint sound of a baby feather fluttering in the wind
        tickles my ear.

"Oh, to be free of tethering,
        like a baby feather on the wind."

North-Eastern Night, 2010.
Watercolour, ink and coloured pencil on hot pressed
90 lb watercolour paper, 5" x 6".
TARA CHARTRAND

XVI.

Upon arrival at Noah's cottage in the woods by the lake,
Chrisna was greeted by a chipmunk welcoming party,
hats and blowers blazing.

~

Later that day,
an Indian red squirrel leapt from the rooftop,
down to the bushes below;
he raced across the dusty path,
and scurried up a stout spruce.

~

At night,
a moth the size of a silver dollar
flew into the cottage.

"Of course, Noah,
we cannot let it breed inside,
but let us not kill."

So, Chrisna beckoned the moth perched on the piano
on the other side of the room.

A flutter,
        but the moth soared over His outstretched hand.

To Noah's surprise,
        the moth landed on His hand,
        with but a second summon;
        its heat radiated through His baby finger.

Thus Chrisna walked to the screen door, slid it open
        and out flew the moth.

XVII.

"One day, along Niagara's shore,
        a grasshopper winked at me,
        its silhouette like a fairy's.

'Have you come here to drink my wine?'
        asked the nimble tumbler.

—Perhaps, noble creature, I said,
        but I prefer to sip the water at the end of this river,
        where its mouth opens wide
        and the divine juice plummets
        to the rocks below."

Mantis, praying, 2010.
Watercolour, ink, and coloured pencil on hot pressed
90 lb watercolour paper, 5" x 6".
TARA CHARTRAND

XVIII.

Once, while waiting for an actress to emerge
from the Festival Theatre,
Vishnu gazed upon a green mantis
crawling through a patch of white pampas grass.

"Oh, my little devout one,
with your hands clasped so,
whatever do you pray for?"

—I pray, my Lord, for these fuzzy patches
to be left in place,
that I may crawl among them all day
to stuff my face with the smaller ones that come my way.

"I dare not refuse a mantis who spends so much time in prayer,
and your plea is fair.

"I shall do my best to fulfil your request."

XIX.

Round and round the seagull flies,
    a huge piece of muffin in his mouth.

From time to time he pauses,
    but the others flock about,
    trying to snatch a morsel of the baked good away.

XX.

Chrisna spied a pudgy green caterpillar squirming along a sidewalk's crack,
  its knobby wobbly body bouncing by and back.

"Oh, my little pea pod,
  where are you off to in such a hurry?"

But, this larva could not yet talk,
  so Chrisna kneeled down and picked it up,
  then placed him in the shade of an elm next to a brownstone
  before rolling off.

XXI.

Lady bugs are always a sign of good luck,
    even if you think everything's fucked.

There's no mood so sour
    that the lady bug's flutter cannot cure.

XXII.

He saw a young girl throwing a fluorescent yellow tennis ball
with her cuddly grey pup,
Her Father watching on,
as a fair white and brown pigeon flew by His frame
to land safe again.

XXIII.

Chrisna flitted through winding halls of water cages
when he chanced upon this scene:

An old walrus peered at the crowd
while bobbing upside-down,
all smiles and whiskers,
his back to the audience,
neck arched back,
and mug crook'd up,
as he blew bubble-kisses
against the glass.

At any time,
a number of young girls
would press themselves against the glass,
pecking the walrus' bubble-kisses back.

But this old walrus,
both dirty and fair,
would from time-to-time run out of air.

So, he would flip his whole body topside-up and front-side front,
exposing the point of his little game,
covering his mystery with all four flippers.

And as he paddled upward for breath,
I pray that you already know the rest,
for though the walrus was the one encased,
he allowed himself a merry escape,
like Leda and the Swan
only in reverse,
without the benefit of intercourse.

XXIV.

“I saw a ‘singer-songwriter’ throat-singing,
 though he wasn’t from Tibet,
 at a coffee shop just on Fairmount,
 somewhere near the bagel shop.

“We witnessed, were shushed,
 derided for not paying attention…

“Where I’m from we use music as a form of prayer;
 we don’t just waffle through the mud
 hoping to breathe life into clay.”

XXV.

"I've been in this linear city for over two weeks,
the country's largest phallus pricking the clouds;
and I haven't seen the sun once.

"Just this grey
that hangs over the city
like a celestial mushroom.

"I look in the mirror.

"My skin has become a sickly shade of bluish-grey,
like a faded print icon of Krishna,
my other self.

"I worry that I'm not getting enough vitamin D,
but I don't blame the city or this country…

"They know no better,
their heads hung, faces frowning
as they walk these acid rain-slicked streets."

XXVI.

“The robust people of this land
        are like the arbutus of the West,
        made both of sun and snow.

“It’s a needleless tree that keeps its leaves
        even in the cold.”

Canadian Mindset, 2010.
Watercolour, ink, and coloured pencil on hot pressed
90 lb watercolour paper, 5" x 6".
TARA CHARTRAND

XXVII.

Who I thought was the squirrel god
was only a god-king.

His Father, a fat yet noble beast;
His coat smoky-white,
His eyes chocolate brown.

No albino this deity
staring me down.

He scampered up a trunk in front of me:

"Our citizens are being expelled from your homes,
from areas between ceiling and roof.

"We ask not much space."

—But to us, having squirrels scratching above is such a disgrace.

"Faux pas, mon ami,
kick out the fucking squirrels.

"We too have our gods."

XXVIII.

A voice was carried to Shiva's ear on the wind:

"The ground is slipping away…"

~

Shiva was whisked away from the city
when he heard a brother's cry.

He flew northward on a maple-grafted airplane,
which landed on a grey strip with banks of snow on either side.

He chartered a sled of huskies, they panting,
glided him to this northern point where ice
sloughs from glacier.

As he arrived to the ocean's edge,
cobbled-stoned by icebergs both large and small,
he leaped from block to block until he arrived at his stop:
the lands of the great polar bear.

—Aaah, Shiva, you heard our cry…

"Fair brother, 'tis not I who destroys your land,
for I only smite evil to make way for Brahma's good,
but now, my love, Vishnu is outstretched."

—Shiva, my lord, we can only swim for so long.

Ice-Ice Shiva 2009.
Watercolour and Gouache, 6" x 9".
COLLEEN MacISAAC

XXIX.

Thus Krishna sang sweetly in Jesus' ear as he hung:

"Babaji, why you instead of me?

"I saw you in my dreams
thousands of years ago too.

"Gods also witness nightmares sometimes,
though my life was a breeze."

Still, Jesus hung.

Thus whispered Krishna to Jesus:

"So you see, Babaji,
my spirit is in you as it is
in all those living."

Babaji, 2009. (modified)
Watercolour and Gouache, 6" x 9".
COLLEEN MacISAAC

XXX.

Kali flew down from the skies
to become a starlet for our age.

She made snuff films,
murdered thousands of bad men,
lopped off their heads,
and turned them into necklace beads.

Everyone watched live on T.V.
for they hated all these men too,
but they loved Kali.

Some still masturbate to Her porn from the earlier days,
when She was still learning how to be human,
doing the whole casting couch thing,
learning how Her body worked,
so slim,
all blue-eyed with milky skin.

But today,
She is a wraith
lusting for slaughter.

We all gushed
when we first saw Her fresh face on cereal boxes,
right before she did Her first few Disney films;
so the turn to porn was a bit of a shock.

She had an interview on Oprah once,
    where She gave a shout out to Heidi Klum
    even though she had gotten Her skin colour wrong,
    but it was a funny moment nonetheless.

She said that the fundamentalists had gone too far
    about that famous Halloween costume;
    personally, I always thought it was brilliant.

She never could stand Dr. Phil though;
    that much was made public.

She had a husband too in the midst of all that—
    that "Shiva" guy,
    a real burn out,
    always talking to himself
    and wandering about aimlessly.

I never really understood what She saw in Him.

He had those ratty dreadlocks
    and he would sometimes wander into the woods
    and cover himself with ash.

He was always throwing those great big bhang parties too;
    all the famous potheads would go:
    Woody Harrelson, Willie Nelson, one of the Wilson brothers...
    you know, the one with the blond hair—
    no, sorry, I meant Matthew McConaughey.

Anyway, He lived in Austin for a while,
was seen sharing a table with Tarentino,
had a rumoured affair with Sandra Bullock,
but that turned out to be bullshit.

But Parvati, let me tell you,
Parvati had the finest ass…

She even got a mainstream acting job or two,
during her porno days,
but those films never really did well—
kind of B comedy stuff.

Now, She's just pitch black,
fourteen feet tall,
Her eyes spewing fire.

Her tongue has forked out like a snake's
as she licks the blood of dead rapists from her lips.

XXXI.

At Barton Springs,
        Chrisna swam crawl between water and sky.

The tips of the plants
        tickled his toes
        as he paddled by.

As he stopped to tread for a moment,
        a Tonkawa chief approached Him
        on a turtle's shell.

"Greetings fair Chrisna!

"How do you fare?"

—Tonkawa elder,
        I was nearly having a mystical experience back there,
        a solar light show just for me.

"I'm so sorry to interrupt."

—Not at all, not at all,
        I had just bobbed up.

"Please, continue your swim,
        and I shall ride upon this turtle's shell."

—Very well. Very well.

The Clown is a Wiseman in Disguise, 2010.
Acrylics on Wood, 66" x 20".
CHRIS DYER

XXXII.

Chrisna walked onto the Hill and asked:

"Why are there no fruits
growing in your parks
while so many go hungry?"

~

Shiva hopped a Vancouver taxi one evening
after smoking a joint at an old friend's.

As they rode through the village,
the driver spoke in a thick Turkish accent,
his throat chaffed from cigarette smoke:

"You see these?

"These are the gays…

"This is their… territory."

Shiva, stoned, knew better than to protest.

Blue Jesus, 2004.
Natural Pigments and Egg Tempera, Gold, Silver on Rabbit Skin Glue and Wood, 6" x 9".
K. GANDHAR CHAKRAVARTY

XXXIII.

In Jesus' time, Chenresi was an ass.
Times were different then.
This too shall pass.

AUTHOR'S ACKNOWLEDGEMENTS

I started working on Maple Vedas back in 2007. I took a much needed break between degrees and several people were kind enough to support this indulgence.

First, thank you Matthew Anderson for your mentorship. Our conversations and revels helped germinate these poems; our ongoing friendship and musings are a happy continuum of this endeavour.

Denise Boudreau and the Young Volunteers of Québec, you run a beautiful programme; thanks again for your confidence. Jean-Pierre Lavallée, thank you for your spirit of benevolence.

Many thanks to the artists who have so graciously contributed their work: Tara Chartrand, Chris Dyer and Colleen MacIssac. You have captured both the levity and the gravity of these poems. Thank you Stephanie North for your lovely suggestion—we went with it. Thanks also to Emery Moreira and the team at 8th House for their relentless attention to detail.

To my family and friends, thank you for your love and patience.

To those who have taken an interest in my poetry:

You give me the temerity to keep writing.

Thank you.

CONTRIBUTING ARTISTS

TARA CHARTRAND was born and raised in Montreal, where she obtained a Bachelor's degree in Design at Concordia University before embracing her first passion, painting and drawing. Her work has been exhibited in several group shows.

CHRIS DYER is a free-lance artist based out of Montreal, known for his colourful detailed spiritual expressions on recycled skateboards. These soulful expressions have been exhibited in solo and group shows in several galleries around the world including San Francisco, New York, Mexico, Peru, Belgium, Paris, and all over Canada and the United States. For more on Chris Dyer's work, please visit: www.positivecreations.ca. Look also for the 2010 release of the feature film about his life and art.

COLLEEN MacISAAC enjoys making comics, illustrations, animations, and theatre. She graduated from the Emily Carr Institute in Vancouver and since then has moved to Halifax where she lives by the sea and tries to spend her time in creative endeavours.

ABOUT THE AUTHOR

K. GANDHAR CHAKRAVARTY is a poet, scholar, and musician. His poems have been published internationally and some have been translated into Bengali, the mother tongue of his most immediate ancestors. *Kolkata Dreams* (2009) represents his first full-length work of poetry, a collection of travel writing developed in 2001. Musically, Gandhar started performing solo when he returned to Montréal after completing a B.A. in English Literature at UWO (2002). This period of his life was punctuated by a number of electro-acoustic nights at Café Sarajevo. In retired music group, Far From Shore (FFS), he was the vocalist, lyricist, and rhythm guitarist. The CD *Wazo* (2006) and the EP *Touch the Sky* (2008) received critical acclaim and the music video for bilingual love song "Amané" was nominated at CraveFest (2007). Gandhar currently performs solo and with impromptu groups and is exploring interactive multilingual non-religious, spiritual hymns that incorporate Indian raga scales. Throughout his artistic endeavours, Gandhar has received two one-year arts grants from the Government of Québec to record music (FFS) and write poetry – *Maple Vedas* (2010). Academically, Gandhar has completed an M.A. in Theological Studies at Concordia University (2007) and he has also published several shorter academic works. He is currently pursuing a Ph.D. in Sciences des religions at Université de Montréal where he is a recipient of the nastional Joseph-Armand Bombardier CGS Doctoral Scholarship (SSHRC). His current studies focus on African Naziritism in Ibandla lamaNazaretha and Rastafari.

www.ingramcontent.com/pod-product-compliance
Lightning Source LLC
Chambersburg PA
CBHW042124080426
42733CB00002B/7

* 9 7 8 1 9 2 6 7 1 6 0 5 3 *